SAMSUNG

GALAXY S9 PLUS
USER MANUAL
FOR **SENIORS**

**Updated Samsung Manual Guide
for Seniors and Beginners**

Stephen W. Rock

Dedicated to all my readers

Acknowledgement

Ii want to say a very big thank you to Michael Lime, a 3D builder, my colleague. He gave me moral support throughout the process of writing this book.

Table of Contents

Introduction

The title of this book already gives a hint on what the book is about. It is a guide for new users of the Samsung Galaxy S9/S9 plus.

Dividing the whole book into three parts, the first part introduces you into how to get started with and explore the Samsung Galaxy S9 and S9 plus, the middle exposes a comprehensive list of tricks and how to execute them, while the last part culminates with useful troubleshooting tips and tricks.

Also, with the comprehensive nature of the book, you'll become a pro in using the Samsung Galaxy devices in less than one hour.

Now, start savoring the content of this book.

Chapter 1

The Samsung Galaxy S9 And The Samsung Galaxy S9 Plus

Samsung Galaxy S9

The Samsung galaxy S9launched on March 2018, comes with a perfect size of 5.80-inch display. It's very comfortable to handle as the curves on the edges makes your hand grasp it very easily. This powerful phone is equipped with a resolution of 2960 x 1440 pixels. It also has a Pixels Per Inch of up to 568 pixels which only means that it is sharper.

The infinity display of the Samsung s9 is amazing as bezel surrounding the screen is made in such a way that the sensors and camera are sort of masked. When looking at the display, you can see the effort taken to make users feel immersed in their screens.

It's true that the size of the display is the same as the s8 but in terms of the AMOLED, it's a lot more powerful. The colors of the screen are way more vibrant and radiantly bright. Imagine watching your favorite Netflix movie on such a screen. In fact, why imagine. Go ahead and try it out. Feel the pleasant experience of display at its best.

The power button as the side is easily accessible just as the Bixby button. The setup at the back of the phone too is a feat in comfortably. The camera of the phone is turned so it can be vertical or straight line with the finger print sensor that's just below it. With this kind of setup at the back, it's a lot easier to reach the fingerprint sensor.

Regarding the full size of the S9, it's a little smaller compared to the S8 but still you till get the same display of 5.8 inch.Which is made possible because of the smallbezels around the screen. And as for the color lovers, you are able to choose between a Lilac Purple, Midnight back, Coral blue and also the Sunrise Gold.

Okay now that's not all this guy can do. It also has a Qualcomm Snapdragon 845 processor. And this incredible chip set offers a wonderful performance. Like for example, apps run and open a lot more quickly, moving your fingers through and swiping around the real estate screen is excellently smooth.

You know those phones that glitch when you're playing games. Or its gets too hot, it feels like there's a cooker in the phone. Well that's because of their crappy processor. But with S9's Snapdragon chipset, the experience is ever so smooth. There are no drawbacks when playing games and it does not become too hot.

With the Samsung Galaxy S9, you are given a 12 megapixel camera. And 12 MP may not sound like a lot, but wait till you actually take photos with it. Or till you shoot in low light. The S9 has variable aperture so that means it is able to adjust between two apertures (f/1.5 with f/2.4)

As with memory, S9 offer a 4Gb RAM and a 64Gb in-built memory. Yu have the ability to insert your own micro SD card. But Samsung offers a seriesof different storage types. You can either opt for the 128GB or the 256GB.

It battery capacity is said to be 3000mAh. And when a recent test was a carriedout, it was shown to last till 6pm after a full day of browsing, playing games and watchingYouTube.

Samsung Galaxy S9 Plus

If you're one looking to buy a smart phone and you've finally settled on the Samsung Galaxy S9 Plus, one of the features you'll be looking forward to is the camera. Who doesn't love a phone with a camera the quality of an eagle's eye. And the Samsung Galaxy S9 Pus is almost as such.

Though they both come with 12 MP rear cameras, the S9 Pus is lot more advanced than the S9 as it is loaded with two camera at the rear. It even features some of Galaxy note 8 features. The lowlight shots are just fantastic.

The camera is set to Auto by default of course. And you can take you're photos like that no problem, but you won't get the most out of your reputable camera. Why don't you just slide right and you'll be in Live focus. What live focus does is that it blurs out the background of the of the photo to give you a nice depth of field in the image.

This is made possible by the dual camera lenses it's armed with. And what's more, three's a slider that allows you fine-tune the blur to your majestic taste.

Like that isn't enough, you can also swipe right from the Live focus and enter pro mode. If you've used a DSLR you will really love this option. It enables you adjust the White balance, focus, exposure, ISO so that you can shoot the finest photo.

Next we've got the super slow motion option. You access this by swiping right from the Auto mode. Once the camera is set to super slow motion, you'll be able to record video at up to 960 frames per second at a resolution of 1280 x 720 pixels. Try it and enjoy the drama. Though you might not get it right the first time, it takes a little time and practice.

What I also love about this phone is the shaved bezel around the screen to give the mode a more modern look. And the display is a bigger than its kid brother the S9. Its size reaches 6.2 inches and is equipped with an AMOLED display of Quad HD+ that is 2960 by 1440 with 529PPI a tad bit more than S9's 570PPI

Here's another area where the S9 plus shows he's senior to the S9. While the S9 shows off its 4GB RAM, the S9 Plus boasts of a RAM of whooping 6GB. If you're one who loves to multitask a lot. This will really come in handy.

Also in terms of battery, the Plus also tops the regular. As S9 Plus has a battery of 3500mAh.

Chapter 2

Preparing Your Samsung S9/S9 Plus

This chapter focuses on helping you get started with your Samsung Galaxy S9/S9 Plus. Many users of the Samsung S series talk about **Intelligent Scan** and **Samsung Pay**. What are they, and how can you use them? Let's consider them at once.

Setting up Intelligent Scan on the Galaxy S9

Let me make this clear; though intelligent scan is a very fast way to unlock your phone, it is not as secure as fingerprint scan or passcode. You may be giving up a bit of your security for convenience. Little wonder you can't use Intelligent Scan to verify mobile payments.

The steps

- ✓ Open the settings app.
- ✓ Tap on Lock Screen and Security.
- ✓ You will see biometrics, under it tap Intelligent Scan. If you do not have a PIN number already, the S9 will ask you to set one up. Once you have done that, tap

'continue' on the verification information screen.

- ✓ In other to register your face, hold your device about 15 inches away with your face centered in the circle on-screen, and tap 'continue'.
- ✓ Register your irises after scanning your face. The S9 advises that you have not glasses and contacts on. You may leave your contacts on if you cannot temporarily do without them.
- ✓ Keep your eyes centered in the on-screen circles. Turn on Intelligent Scan after registering your face and irises.
- ✓ Ensure that Intelligent Scan unlock and Screen-on Intelligent Scan are toggled on. This will make it possible to quickly unlock your phone without needing to swipe the screen first.

Do not sign up for crappy cloud services. Google's free cloud services do a wonderful job storing your data, contacts, and photos- naming a few. So you should avoid subscribing to any other limited-size clod services.

Setting up Samsung Pay on the Galaxy S9

Samsung galaxy pay is a mobile wallet service that is offered by Samsung for its mobile devices. The essence of this innovation is to replace the plastic card in your wallet. This service currently is available in the United States, United Kingdom, Singapore, India, and many other countries of the world. To enable this feature on your S9 device, consider the following steps;

1. Open Samsung Pay and tap get started to proceed.
2. Once Samsung Account set up is complete, tap on the Samsung Pay icon and then register your fingerprint by tapping 'use Fingerprint.'
3. Register a Samsung Pay PIN that will be used for authenticating payments in the future. Then tap add Credit/Debit card or Membership card; it all depends on which you want to use with Samsung Pay.
4. The camera will opens within the app. You'll need to use it to auto read your card details. If you like, you can add the details manually.
5. Samsung Pay will prompt you to verify your identity through an OTP which you will receive through an SMS. If you 're unable to see the SMS option, simply select 'Call Bank' for a tele-verification by customer care team just before you register.

In the next chapter, when I'd be highlighting solutions to common problems faced by Samsung Galaxy S9 users, I'd teach you some tricks for solving 'Samsung Pay not working' problem.

Compatible Galaxy S9/S9 Plus apps to explore

The following apps will help you optimize your Samsung phone. They are both essential and compatible with your device.

- AR GPS compass map 3D
- Field trip
- SmartThings app
- Amazon Kindle
- GBoard
- Bacon camera
- sesame Shortcuts
- adBlockers
- Rocket Player
- Google translate
- Quiver
- MX player
- Google Duo
- Unified Remote
- SMS Organizer
- Authy
- Newpipe
- PSPP – PSP Emulator

- Xender
- Tiny Scanner
- Samsung Max
- Feedly- Get Smarter

Tips for improving Samsung Galaxy Battery Life

Poor battery life isn't want you desire for your costly phone. No matter the quality of features your Samsung Galaxy S9/S9 Plus has, if it has a poor battery life, you won't be able to derive real satisfaction from it. So how can you improve your battery's life? Well the following bulletin points have practically worked for me and should be taken seriously.

1. Turn off always on display
2. Stop apps from running in the background
3. Adjust screen timeout
4. Lower Screen Resolution
5. Lower display brightness

Chapter 3

Samsung Galaxy S9 and S9 Plus Tips and Tricks.

Increase Your Display Resolution.

Did you know that your Samsung Galaxy s9 and S9 plus has an OLED Infinity Display of 2960 by 1440 resolution. Yeah your phone can give you a display as high as that. And also the accuracy of the color and the brightness too is top notch.

But your phone doesn't switch to such quality automatically. But that's because it wants to save battery. But if that's none of your business, here's how you can switch it higher.

1. Enter **Settings**
2. Go to **Display Settings**
3. Then **Screen resolution**

Control Color Balance Of S9

It's no lie that the Samsung Galaxy S9 screen is beautiful and smart. Smart in the sense that it can adjust the sharpness, saturation, color of the display according to what you're doing on the phone.

You also have the capability of changing the color range to suit your taste.
1. Go to **Settings**
2. Then **Display**
3. Select **Screen mode**.

You can tap the **Advanced options** if you want to tweak the color of the display manually. Or you can just move the slider to adjust the display and make it warmer or maybe you prefer cooler.

Secure Your Files.

Almost everyone has a folder that he doesn't want anyone lurking around in. If you're that kind and you want to safeguard your tremendously private files so that no one can see, Just open a secure folder.

Yes, with this you are able to preserve your sensitive files and keep it safe and locked. To open a secure folder
1. Open up the **Settings**
2. Go to **Lock Screens And Security**
3. Select **Secure Folder**.
4. Then **Next**.

Before you can confirm you have to log in to your Samsung account.

Do Not Disturb

There just some times when you don't want to be bothered by anything, no notifications, no calls. Just you alone in peaceful land. Or maybe there are some annoying apps that you wish to silence. That's the time you switch to **Do Not Disturb**

Of course the **Do Not Disturb** option is not enabled automatically, you will have to do that yourself.

1. Go to **Settings**.
2. Select **Sounds And Vibration**
3. Tap **Do Not Disturb**
4. Turn on **Do Not Disturb**

You can also silence some specific calls by
1. Selecting **Sounds And Vibration** in **Settings**
2. **Do Not Disturb**
3. Then choose **Allow Exceptions**.
4. If you select **Custom**, you are able to allow only certain calls

Use Dual Audio Option

Another lovely feature of the S9 series is the **Dual Audio**. What Dual Audio does is that it enables you be able to send audio to two headset using Bluetooth at once. As long as you paired the two Bluetooth head phones to your S9 all you have to do is just switch on Dual Audio

1. Enter your **Settings**
2. Select **Connections**
3. Choose **Bluetooth**
4. Touch three dot symbol at the top corner of the page
5. Hit **Dual Audio**
6. Toggle on **Dual Audio**.

The Live Focus

Here is something I just love about the S9 Plus. Is its dual camera. This allows you to adjust aperture, use optical zoom, reduce the noise in images and even add a classy bokeh

The one that's really making me drool is the Live focus that allows you to blur the area of the background to give you a depth of field effect on your photos.

The dual camera of the S9 Plus comes with 12MP. You are able to shoot with $f/1.5$ wide angle lens with one of the cameras. And the other camera gives you a $f/2,4$ telephoto lens.

To switch to live focus, just swipe right

Change The Aperture Manually

Still on the awesome camera of the S9 series. This one's the ability to control the aperture of the camera. By default, the camera adjusts the aperture based on the lighting condition, either dark or sunny.

But you have the ability to manually control the aperture. This is made available in the Pro mode. To do this just swipe left twice and select the aperture symbol. To show that aperture is active, you should see a button at the downside of the screen if you're using landscape mode. It is in this area that you are able to change between f/2.4 or f/1.5

Reply To Message While In An App.

There's this cool option that's available in the S9. It's the ability to respond to messages while still in an app. Texting back to someone can be a bit tiring when you're busy in an app or game. You don't want to leave the person hanging and you don't want to quit your game also.

And it can be a bit stressful closing all your progress in an app just to reply to one message.

Well in the S9 there's a way you can reply while still operating an app. All you do is swipe down from top of the display in the app you're in and enlarge the window.

Enabling One Handed Mode

Many say the S9 is small but it's still big compared to other phones. And with the introduction of giant 6.2 inch S9 plus the One Handed Mode is like a must.

The S9 plus is big and it can be really aching to try and type throughout he wide screen with one hand when the other is busy with something

Samsungs got you well covered on this. They've created the one handed mode to ease the stress. This option makes the screen display smaller for it to be a lot easier to navigate with just one hand.

To enable this,
1. Fire up the **Settings**
2. Touch **Advanced Settings**.
3. Select **One Handed Mode**.

Enable Dolby Atmos

Ever heard of Dolby Atmos? Well it's a technology that gives you stereo separation as you watch videos and a possibility of increased volumes. Just like other cool features, this too is available on the S9 and S9 plus but it's switched off by default so you'll have to turn it on.
To do this,
1. Enter **Settings**
2. Move to **Sounds And Vibration**
3. Select **Sound Quality And Effects**
4. Click **Dolby Atmos** and toggle it on
5. Select **Auto** or any other preferred choice

The Super Slow-Mo

So there is this cool new feature in Samsung Galaxy phones that we are totally loving. It is the power of super slow-mo. As the name implies, this is the ability for the phone to shoot in slow-motion. And with the S9 it's not just any slow-mo, this is 960 frames per second (you won't find this in other top brands).

What's more, the fact that it is in super slow mo doesn't mean the quality is any lower. You get a stunning resolution of up to 1280 x 720 pixels.

To get to this awesome feature, you swipe left from your camera. If you click the **Settings** and choose **Super Slow-Mo**, there will be an option to shoot based on the movement of several items or just one.

To view and share the video, move over to **Gallery**. But you should remember, shooting in Super Slow-Mo will take up 20MB per second. So if you're using the 64GB storage, it can quickly be filled up. It would do you much good if you get a microSD card to supplement.

Increase Touch Sensitivity

Oh yeah I know that feeling of try to tap on something in your screen but it just wouldn't click, at least not until you pressed it 4 times. And trust me it only gets worse with screen protectors. Some make it a harder to touch the screen and get a response.

During those disheartening times all you do is increase the touch or screen sensitivity of your phone.

As the name implies, this increases the way your phone is sensitive to touch. To do this,

1. Go to **Settings**
2. Select **Advanced Features**
3. Choose **Touch sensitivity**.

Use Bixby To Search Your Location.

We all know Bixby, the Samsung digital assistant. It's been deeply rooted in the S9 and Plus camera. As it employs Augmented Reality, it uses it to provide useful information from all around the world.

When you direct your phones camera at an item, Bixby scans and offers facts regarding the object. And it can even add a translation that translates signs that are written in unfamiliar languages form you to understand.

As you open camera, select Bixby vision that's by the lower corner on the left side. Then point your phone to what you wish to translate as you press the T sign. Once you do that, it will transform the language to the language you phone is set to, to the one you understand.

To adjust this,
1. Go to **Bixby Home**
2. Then **My Bixby**.

Save More Battery On The S9

It's true that the battery of the Samsung Galaxy S9 is 3000mAh. It will work well but may not really last long depending on your usage. But there's something you can do to conserve your battery.

Like using the device maintenance setting. This will help the battery from sucking away rather quickly. You do this by;

1. Going to **Settings**
2. Then **Device Management**
3. Select **Battery**

Opening the section of Battery Usage, you are able to see all the details of how your battery is being used.
If you select **Power saving mode**, you will be able to lengthen the life of your battery

Another feature that you will find useful is the App Power monitor. This will enable you to force apps that are not used much to sleep. When you do this, they will be rendered harmless and not be able to suck away battery. If you choose the unmonitored apps, you will be able to leave out some app that you don't want to force to sleep

You also have the ability to setup more by going to the advanced settings for battery.
1. Select **More Options**
2. Choose **Advanced Settings**

Edit The Message App.

In your Samsung Galaxy S9, you have the power to change the display of the Messages. To edit, all you do is alter your theme in your S9 and change the Settings of the font.

If you want to change the Themes,
1. Press and hold any area that's empty on the homescreen.
2. Select view all to see all the themes available.
3. Choose the theme you want
4. Tap Apply.

In case the list for default themes doesn't not suit your royal taste, you can always download.

Utilize The Dual Messenger

The dual messenger feature available on the S9 allows you to have two accounts on apps of messenger, like Facebook, Whatsapp, Viber, Snapchat, WeChat and the likes. You be able to run two messenger accounts all together at the same time.

If you're one that uses several accounts, then this is like good news. With dual messenger you be able to down another version of the same messenger so that you can turn two accounts and easily switch.

You enable this feature by
1. Going to **Settings**
2. Select **Advanced Features**.
3. Then **Dual Messenger**.

If you're coming from Note 8 then this is not new to you. But as for we mere humans, we are loving this feature on our S9.

Switch Homescreen To Horizontal Mode.

Your S9 is set to portrait mode by default. Cause that's how it should be. But if you're one that doesn't fancy that and love the landscape mode better, there's a sweet feature that allows you view the content of the screen when it's set horizontally.

You set this by,
1. Going over to the **Settings**.
2. Selecting **Display**,
3. Clicking **Homescreen**
4. Find the **Portrait mode only** and turn it off

Once that is done, you will be able to turn your phone around to landscape and the orientation would you be accurate. As expected since your changing the view, some widgets might not show the same way it used to with portrait.

Using AR Emojis

Things will definitely not be normal if I didn't mention this cool feature. Some call it creepy actually. If you're new to the Samsung party, AR Emoji is a camera function that allows you to build an emoji version of yourself. You can even change your skin tone, glasses or hair, it's up to you.

To use AR emoji,
1. Open the **Camera**
2. Switch to the front camera
3. In the options at the top of the screen, select **AR Emoji**. If you don't see it, swipe the options
4. Select the face icon that's at the bottom of the display
5. Then **Create Emoji**
6. Make sure your face in centred in the viewfinder and nothing is blocking your face, even your glasses or hair.
7. After answering if you're a male or female, your avatar will be created and you'll be able to make changes as you wish.

Arm Yourself With Selfie Focus

Both on the Samsung Galaxy S9 and S9 Plus users have the ability to use their front-facing camera and switch to Selfie focus.

The awesome thing about Selfie focus is the blurry effect it gives. Once your face is well centred in the circle, your face will be crisp and sharp while any other will be blurred. In fact you have the ability to fine-tune skin tones when you click on the circle that's below on the side.

Don't edit your face too much; remember Too much of everything is not good. Do it moderately and watch as you're face switches from normal to charming

Using The Optical Zoom

You know your Samsung Galaxy S9 Plus has dual lens right? And thanks to this, we have **2x Optical Zoom**. You have the ability to select anyone you wish after you position the camera to take both.

To shoot in 2x Optical Zoom all you do is look for **2x** on the screen. It's on the right at the bottom. Once you select 2x, it will switch to 1x. Select the 1x if you want to go back to normal view.

Or you can just press with your fingers and expand to zoom. But if you zoom too much, you'll exceed 2x Optical Zoom and enter digital zoom. And the quality of the image will surely be low.

Top Notch Phone Security

With the Samsung Galaxy S9 series, PIN code or pattern securities are cavemen in the Stone Age. S9 and S9 Plus has one of the leading technology for phone security. As it uses your iris, face and fingerprint to unlock your phone.

First you'll need to setup your PIN,
1. Dig in the **Settings**
2. Scroll and Tap **Lock Screen and Security**.
3. Then **Screen Lock Type**
4. Select **PIN** and set it up. Be sure to use a complex PIN that you'll remember. You really shouldn't forget this PIN. It's like the key to all the doors in your phone.

Now if you prefer Fingerprint.
1. Go to **Settings**
2. Click **Lock Screen And Security**
3. In the **Biometrics** section, Select **Fingerprint Scanner**
4. You'll be asked to input your **PIN**
5. Choose **Add Fingerprint** and follow the prompts

Or you like the sound of **Intelligent Scan** and want to try it out

1. Select **Intelligent Scan** Under **Biometrics**
2. Hit **Continue**
3. Obey the instruction it gives diligently and set your phone in front of your face in proper lighting.
4. Now you set your iris. Remove any glasses or contact to do this.
5. Now turn on **Intelligent Scan**. And Verify that **Screen-on Intelligent Scan** and **Intelligent Scan unlock** are both turned on.

Save Time With The Split Screen

One awesome feature in the Samsung Galaxy S9 and S9 Plus is the ability to split the display of the phone so that you can make two apps run simultaneously. Multitasking, eh?

If you want to equip yourself with this, go to the Multi-Window pane and verify that **Pop-Up View Action** is turned on.

Next you'll go to the button for **View recently used apps**. Slide downwards and choose the multi-window symbol that's on the window for recent app. The application you want to launch will open window at the top. You and choose a different app that will run in he other window

Turn Up Your Game With Samsung DeX

Samsung Galaxy S9 and S9 Plus is said by some to offer every feature on earth. And I'm kinda believing that fact. I mean why wouldn't you . When a phone says it can connect itself through a cable to your PC, you have to agree Samsung made it big with S9 and S9 plus.

Once you connect your phone to the monitor of the computer you be able to control it using a normal mouse and keyboard.

To use the DeX mode, you will need a DeX pad or a DeX station. As long as you connect the cables properly, everything should be fine and Samsung DeX should begin automatically.

Bring Back The App Drawer.

If you've just moved from an older Android to Samsung Galaxy S9 then you would probably miss the app drawer button. Who needs an app drawer button anyway if you've got swiping? But actually some do. They just love that white icon that sits on their homescreen. And if you're one of those guys, here how to bring the app drawer back.

1. Press and hold on an empty area on your display. Just like if you want to change your wallpaper.
2. Select the **Settings icon**.
3. Touch the feature called **Apps Button**
4. Choose **Show Apps Button**

Enable Smart Lock

Wait, so locks can be smart? Well, Yes. Though not just any Android, it's the S9 and S9 Plus that has this capability. We just talked about setting up intelligent scan, sure intelligent scan is nice and useful but what I'm just totally adoring now is the Smart lock feature.

What this does is that it turns off the security in your phones when you get to a certain location that you set. Once you get to a place that you set is safe, your phone will unlock. Cos why would you need to use tight lock security when you're home relaxing with your partner. They wouldn't steal your phone.

With this feature, you don't have to bother about unlocking your phone when you're home. But when outside in the danger zone of the unknown, that's when you need that heavy duty security that your S9 can give you.

To use this,
1. Go to **Settings**
2. Select **Lock And Security**
3. Then **Smart Lock**
4. Obey the onscreen instruction it provides

Move apps to the Galaxy S9 MicroSD Card

No doubt, the S9/S9+ has a huge memory space, but wait a year or two and see how slow-motion or 4k videos, apps, tons of games, music and movies will take up that space. You then realize the need to move apps to the microSD. Funny enough, this isn't hard to do. How can this be done?

1. Head to **Settings** > **Apps** > **All Apps**
2. Select an App from the list and tap on the third option labeled **Storage**
3. Where it says 'Storage used, internal storage' click the **Change button**
4. Choose **MicroSD** from the pop-up menu
5. Select **Move** at the bottom right, and wait for it to export

Repeat steps for any other eligible app you want to move

Try doing these only when you begin to run out of space.

Use the night mode

Did you know that the blue light from the screen can cause eye strain and keep one awake? Well, the S9/S9 plus has this feature that turns off some blue colors on the display.

You enable this and you'll reduce the risk of eye strain and you should go to sleep faster.

Just go to

1. **Settings**
2. Then **Display**
3. Select **Blue Light Filter**

You can customize when it comes on and off or how strong it is.

Disable bloat ware on the Samsung Galaxy S9

A bloat ware is simply a pre-installed app that you may never use; it's just there wasting space. It's impossible to uninstall these apps, but you can disable them. That way none of them will ever appear in the application tray, on your home screen, or waste time updating on Google Play. How can a bloat ware be disabled? The following steps will help you:

1. Pull the notification bar down and hit the gear-shaped Settings button (or simply open the settings app).
2. Navigate to and select Apps (ensure the tab on the top left says All Apps).
3. Scroll through the list of apps and select any app you want to disable.
4. Tap **Disable**, then **Confirm** to get rid of the app (some apps will need to uninstall updates first before they get disabled).
5. Repeat steps **3 and 4** for any other app you want to disable.

These actions will be great for unused apps like AT&T WiFi, Sprint's NASCAR apps, Lookout, Hancorn Office, Verizon, T-Mobile, etc.

Open a secure folder

Are you someone that likes to keep super confidential files that no other person should ever set eyes on? Then the S9's got you covered in the area of security.

You can create a 'Secure Folder that will allow you to store private and confidential documents or items in a secure place.

All you do is visit

1. **Settings**
2. **Lock Screen and Security**
3. Then **Secure Folder**
4. Choose **Next, Start**

Log in to your Samsung account and hit **Confirm**

Now you need an authentication method to access the folder. You can use a PIN, pattern, password. But be careful. Make it as tight as possible.

I've seen passwords people use that a 5-year-old would have no problem guessing. So try to use a different password. That you've never used. That no one knows.

You do that and your secure folder will be like a gate firmly sealed with a heavy padlock

Change fonts

Have you ever watched from the sidelines how the big boys use fonts to style their text and make their phone look awesome? Well, no more are you going to be the spectator as you'll see how to change fonts on the S9.

And you know what, it's damn easy. Just hit

1. **Settings**
2. Select **Display**
3. Then **Screen zoom and font**.

Select one to use. If they all don't suit you, you can download a new one. Apply it and you're the big boy.

Amp up your display resolution

Normally, Samsung has set the display to 1080p Full HD by default. And it's for good reason as a lower resolution can save battery.

But if you just don't give a damn and want the sweet resolution you're entitled to, head over to

1. **Settings**
2. Select **Display**
3. Then **Screen resolution**

Slide right and choose your 2560x1440 WQHD+. This resolution is perfect for movies and games.

Schedule software updates

How do you feel while using your phone and then immediately you're connected to a Wi-Fi, apps and programs start updating automatically?

It can be frustrating, right? Yeah, I know. Been there, felt that.

But there's good news. You can actually set a time for software updates.

To do this, simply hit

1. **Settings**
2. Select **Software Updates**
3. Then **Scheduled Software Updates**

Choose your desired time and you're golden.

Camera quick launch

There's no way I would forget this shortcut. I should have mentioned it earlier. Now, this one's a sweet secret. It's the trick to launch the camera rather quickly.

And it's like the easiest thing to do. Just quickly press the **power button** twice and you're in camera. It works anywhere you are on the phone either **home screen**, an app, or even when the screen turns dark.

But if for some reason, this doesn't work, simply hit **Settings** in **Camera->** Swipe down and toggle **Quick launch** on

Chapter 4

Galaxy S9/ S9 Plus Apps Problems And Solutions

As impressive as the Samsung Galaxy S9 is, there are issues that can arise. Remember, these devices aren't perfect. That is why I took time to search forums, comments, and news to look for common problems with the Galaxy S9 and S9 Plus, and how to fix them.

Let us discuss them accordingly.

Smearing around black objects/black crush

Some users have complained that black areas in media and images are failing to blend properly with other colors, resulting in areas that look pixelated, blurred, or just completely odd

The Solution:

There has been an update, so make sure your phone is fully updated if you're still getting the problem. Simply hit Settings > System updates > Check for system updates to make sure.

Dead zone on the touchscreen

I have come across complaints from users on Samsung's official forums and so many Reddit threads that sections of the touchscreens on their S9s are not responding to their touch. In many cases, the dead area appears to be a band laid horizontally across the device and isn't in the same place for each person. Some users have tried to resolve the issue through factory resets and altering sensitivity options in the phone's settings, but the problem still persists.

The Solution:

This is a hardware issue, so the first thing you should do is to speak to whomever you bought the device from and get it fixed or replaced under your warranty. If you got it directly from Samsung, it asked affected users to contact them directly at 1-800-Samsung.

Samsung Messages app has sent my entire gallery to a random contact

I have come across a lot of users of the S9 lamenting that their entire gallery of images has been sent to another contact, with no sign on their side that this had occurred. Although the impact seems to have been minimal so far, this is a bug that could result in your inconvenience. It seems the most affected people are those who are on T-Mobile and share a plan with other Galaxy device users.

The Solution

Since the issue affects only Samsung Messages, simply revoke that app's ability to access your storage. To do so;

1. Open **Settings apps**

2. Hit **Samsung Messages App> Permissions** , and then revoke the Storage permission.

Keep in mind that taking this action   will probably make your Samsung Messages app unusable, so you should download an alternate messaging app before taking action.

Very dark super slow-motion video

Is super slow-motion video showing up with dramatically increased levels of darkness in lower lighting conditions? This bug does not affect all users of the S9, but if it affects your device, then you will notice a contrast in the lighting between your Auto camera mode and when you switch to your Super Slow-Motion mode.

The Solution:

The problem has been acknowledged by Samsung and is working on software to correct it. If this bug affects you, be patient.it should be fixed by Samsung soon.

Bluetooth not pairing to device

A whole lot of users have complained about intermittent connection problems including an inability to pair, periodic drops in connection, and inability to reconnect to car-based Bluetooth systems.

A possible solution

If you're having problems getting your S9/S9 Plus to pair with other Bluetooth devices, ensure you try running through Samsung's directions on possible Bluetooth problems. If the problem persists try holding down the Bluetooth's power for long to be sure you've entered pairing mode. If that doesn't help also, endeavor to reach out to Samsung for help.

If your S9 Plus isn't reconnecting to your car's Bluetooth system like your previous device used to, it might be that your previous phone is still listed in your car's connection. The S9 Plus may not connect. You may have to remove my older phone from the list before the connection can smoothen.

Can't record voice calls

Many users have complained that no matter which call-recording software is used, the S9 will only pick up one side of the conversation, and will not record the person on the other end of the call.

The Solution:

According to reports gathered from Samsung EU forums , call recording is blocked on the S9 and S9 Plus in order to meet Google's security policies and local laws in the EU. These processes were specially built up on the Galaxy S9 and S9 Plus.

Samsung Pay not working; fixing the problem

There are lots of users facing some problems while trying to use Samsung Pay. And the feeling can be dejecting. Do not worry, I'll help you on how to fix the most prominent problems encountered with the Samsung Pay. Whether your device pops up 'incompatible app' or otherwise, you can fix the problem by following the suggestions below.

1. **Samsung has acknowledged the issue** and have rolled out a new bug fixing update. A new patch of the app is available on the App store. So head to the App store and tap on the patch button. Also, ensure that you have the firmware for the Samsung Pay country you are in. The app would not run if otherwise. So be sure the firmware matches with your own country.

2. **Restart the phone.** To do this, simply tap on the power button for a few seconds till the options pop on the screen. Tap on the 'power off' and press 'OK'.

3. **Reset Samsung Pay.** This is also another useful trick that can work if the cause of the mal function isn't a bug. To do this, just go to Samsung Pay, tap on the 'sign in' option at the upper right corner. Select 'forget password'. Enter your mail ID.

Type the security code and wait for a mail with the new password.

4. **Remove and add a new card.** This also is another trick for solving the problem. To utilize this trick, consider the following steps;

    1. Open the Samsung Pay and tap on the Credit/Debit card option
    2. Select which card you want to add or remove
    3. Tap on 'more option' and select 'delete card'.
    4. Verify the Samsung PIN and you are good to go.

The above method can be followed if you want to add a new card.

Camera failed error; fix it

If this problem is a result of a minor app glitch, simply restarting the camera app may be all you need to do. To do this, consider the below easy steps.

1. Tap and hold the 'Recent apps' key at the bottom left corner of your phone. This will open a new screen containing your most recently used apps.
2. Close all the apps.
3. If this doesn't work, go to settings and select camera app in the Apps list and then clear cache.

If the above steps still do not bring the desired result, boot into safe mode and diagnose the apps. Sometimes, third party apps can cause conflicts and trigger errors in other apps. Try doing the following;

1. Turn off your phone. Press and hold the power button past the model name screen showing on the screen.
2. Release the button when the Samsung logo appears and immediately hold the volume down button. Keep holding until your device finishes restarting.
3. When you see the 'safe mode' badge on the bottom left corner of the screen, you can release the 'volume down button'.

It is now time to launch the camera app. Try taking photos or recording videos. If the initial error is not encountered while in safe mode, it means the third-party app is to blame. Think of the third-party apps you downloaded and uninstall them immediately.

Otherwise, you should update camera app and/or your Samsung S9 to the latest software version.

Disclaimer

In as much as the author believes beginners will find this book helpful in learning how to use the Samsung Galaxy S9/S9 plus, it is only a small book. It should not be relied upon solely for all Samsung tricks and troubleshooting.

About the author

Stephen Rock has been a certified apps developer and tech researcher for more than12 years. Some of his 'how to' guides have appeared in a handful of international journals and tech blogs. He loves rabbits.

Facebook page @ Techgist